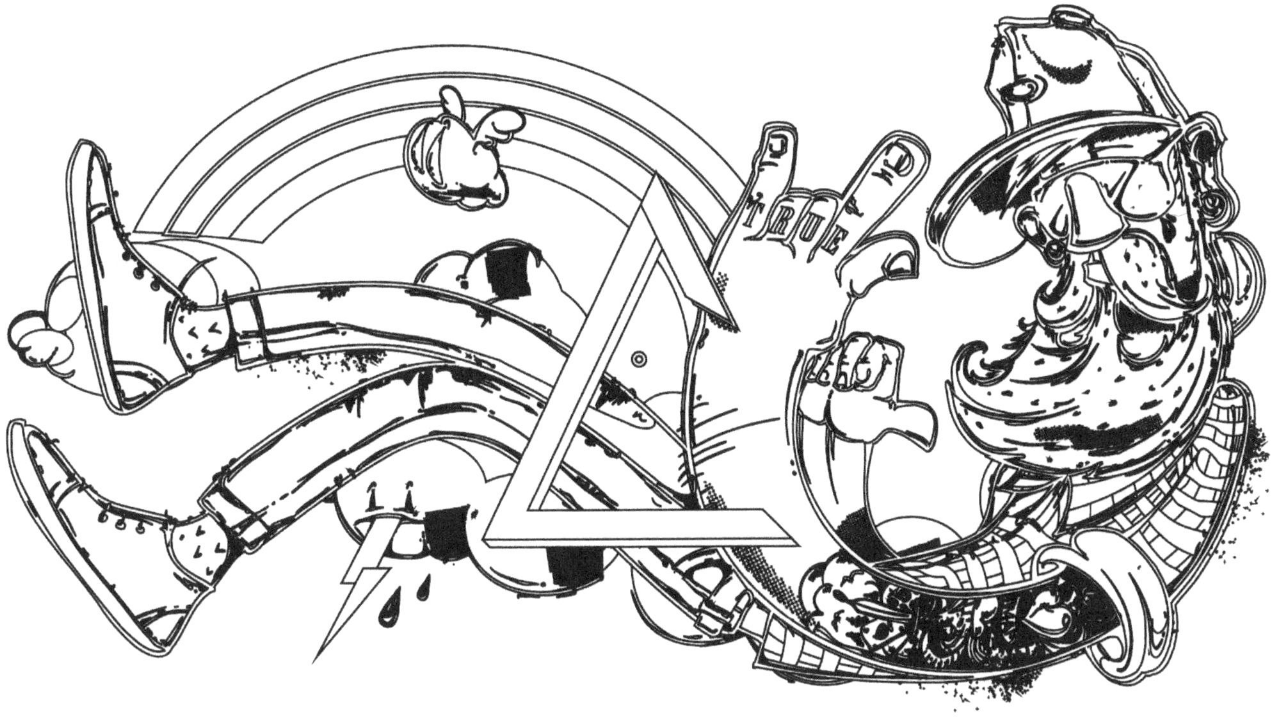
TRUE

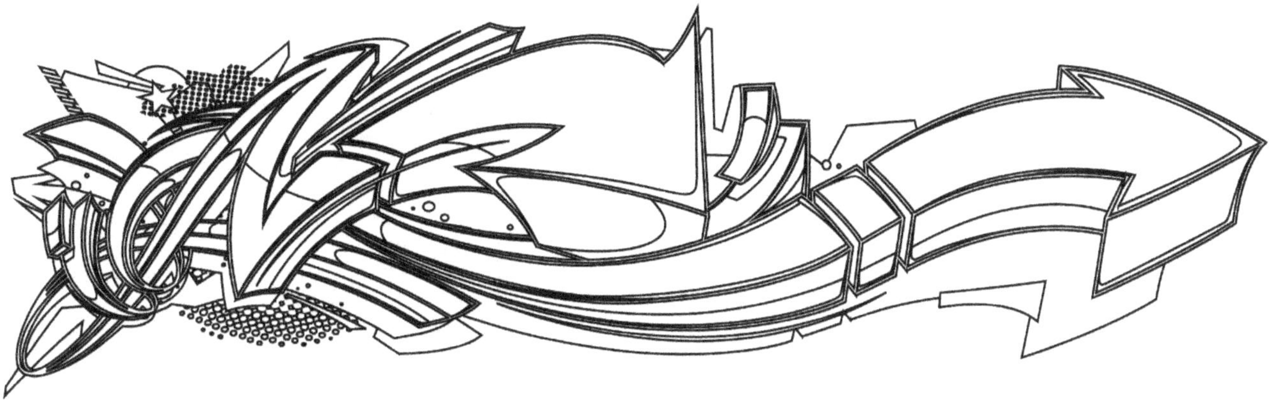

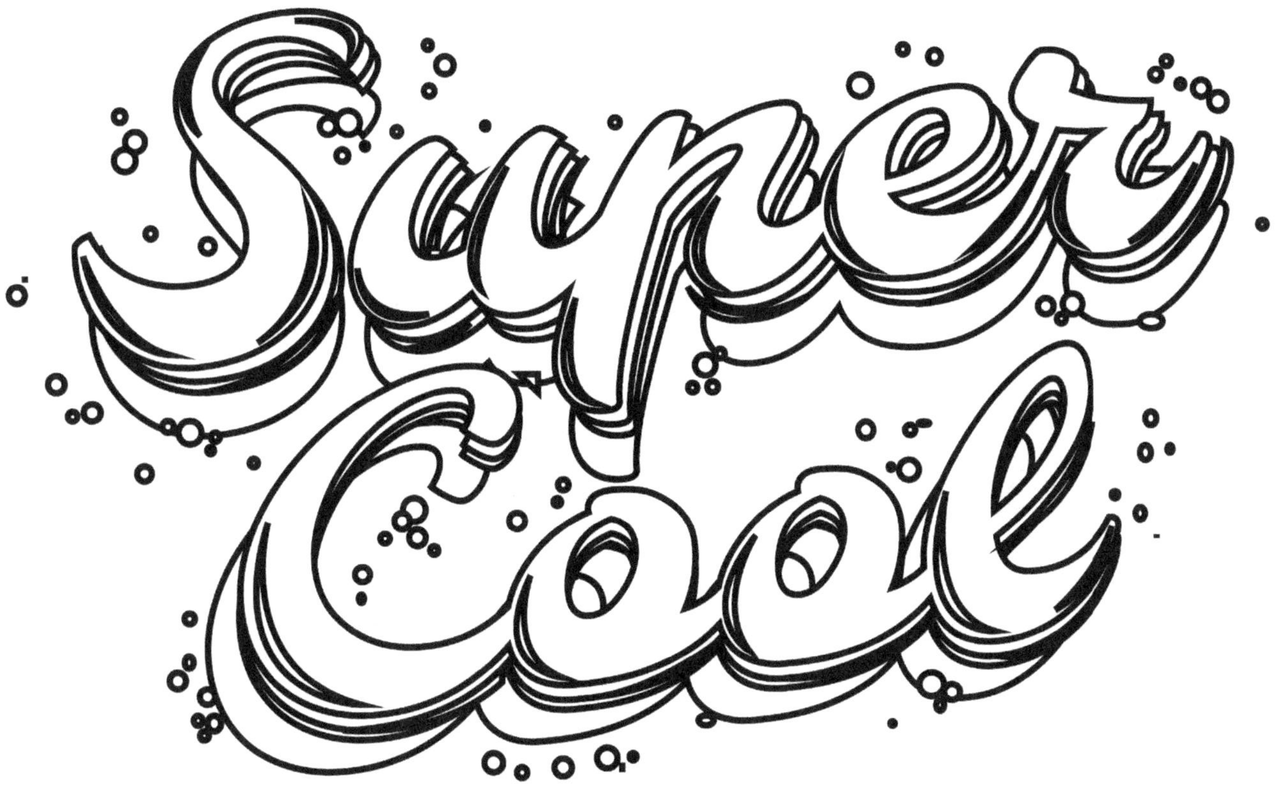
Super
Cool

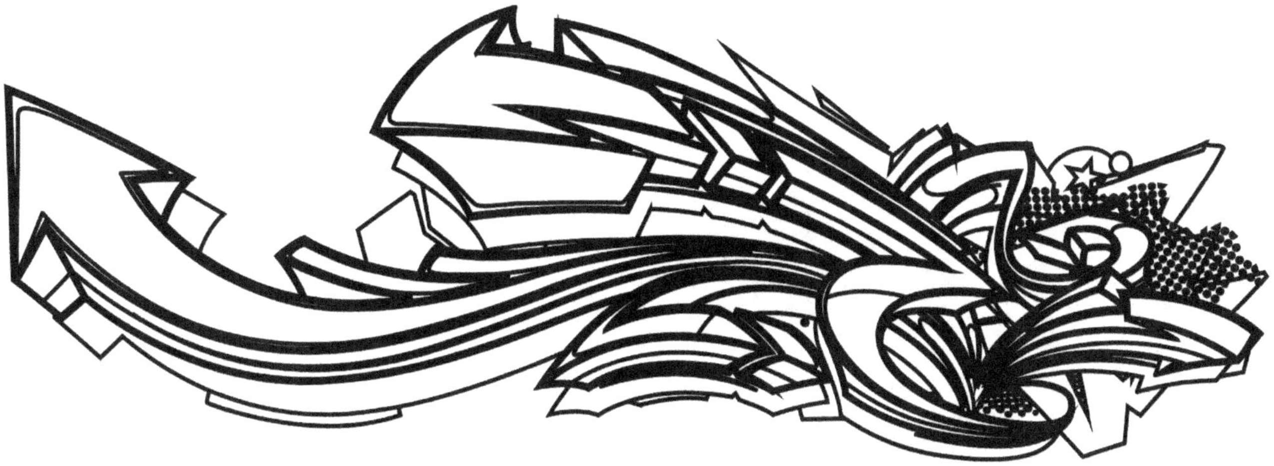

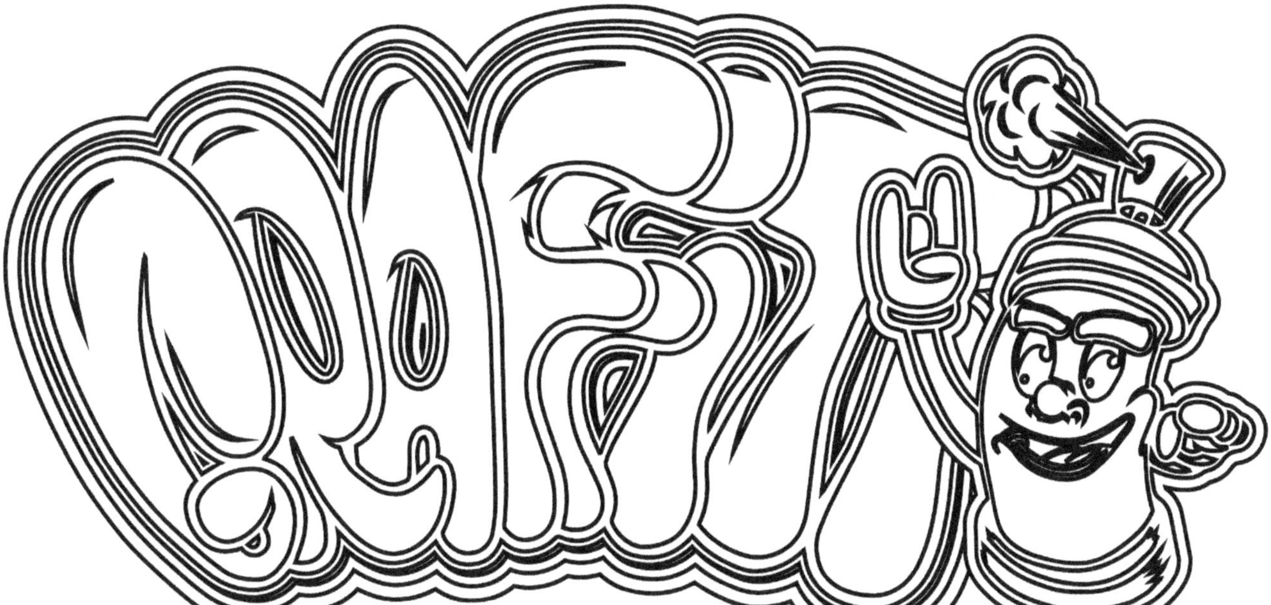

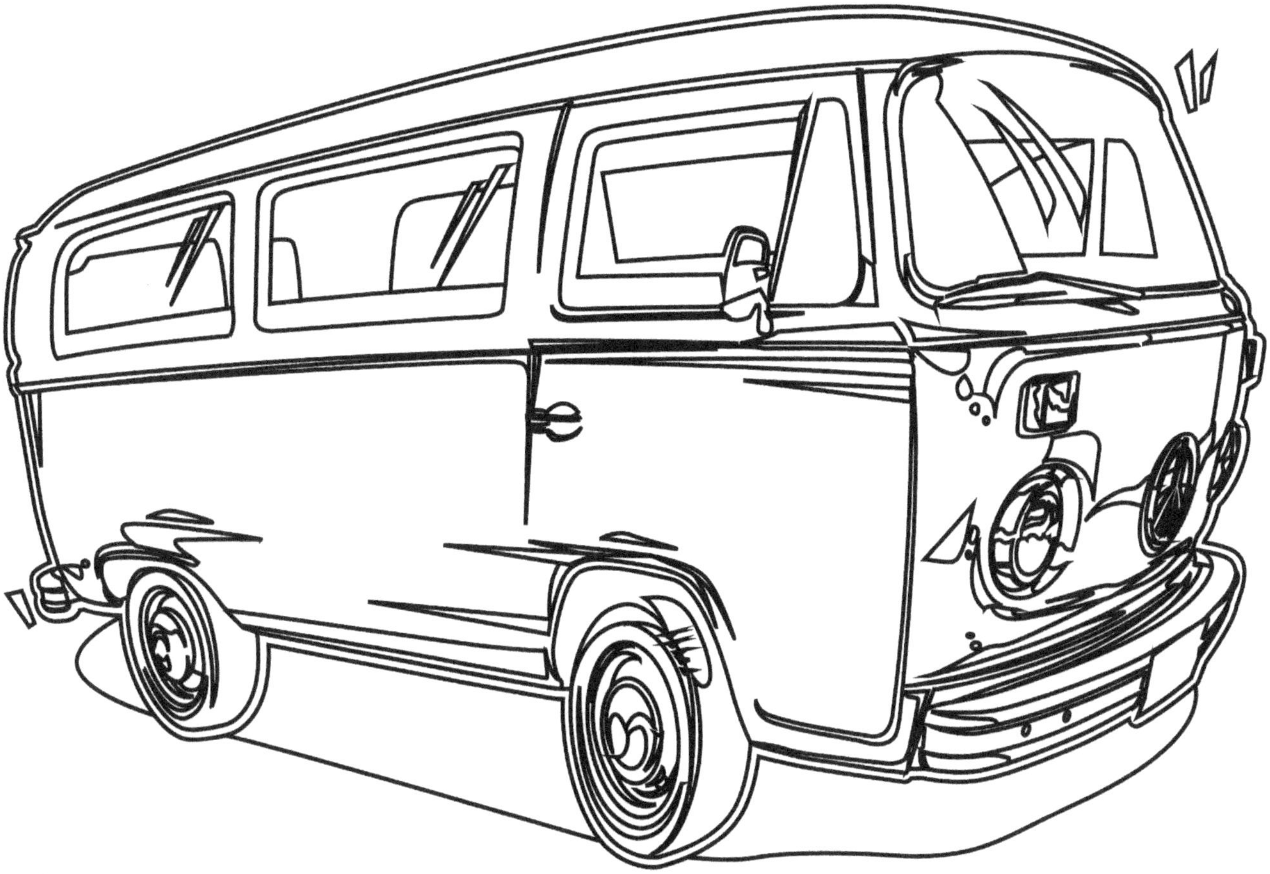

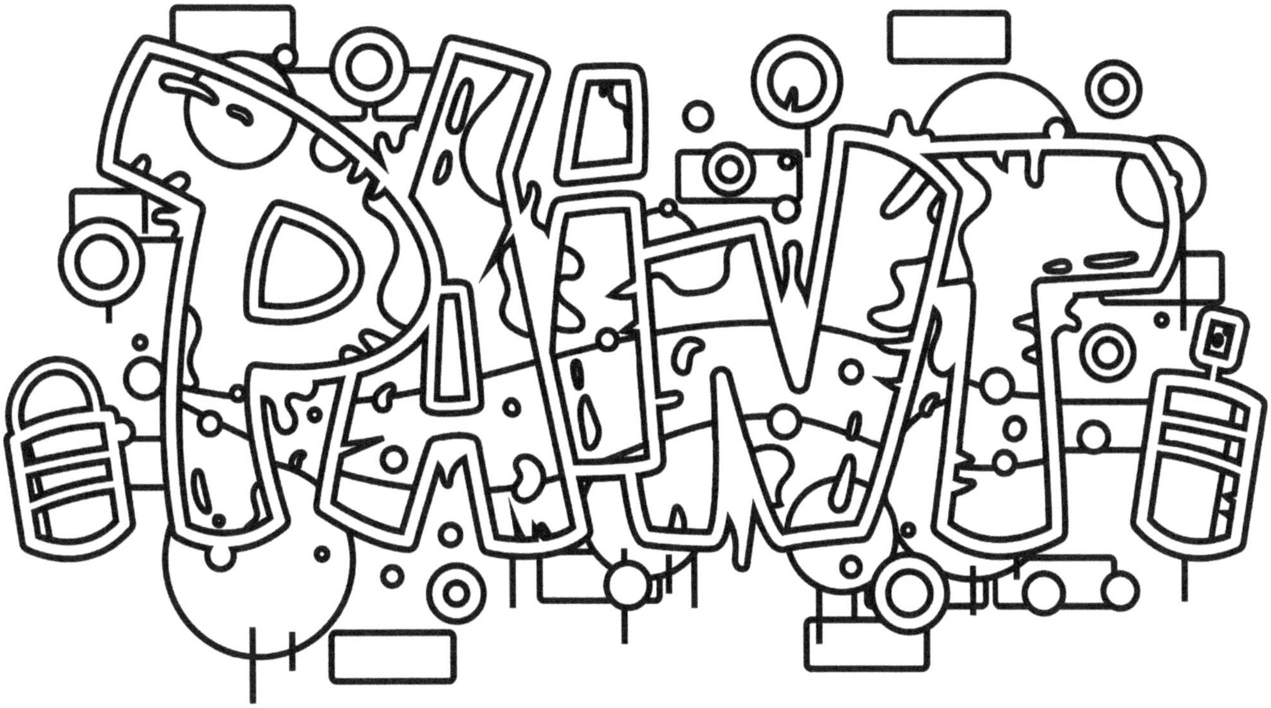
PAINT

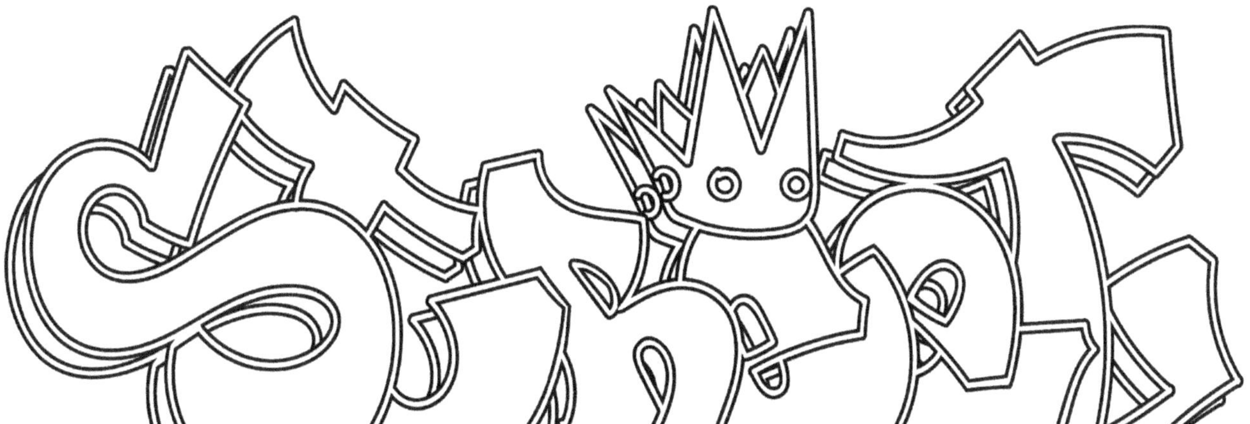

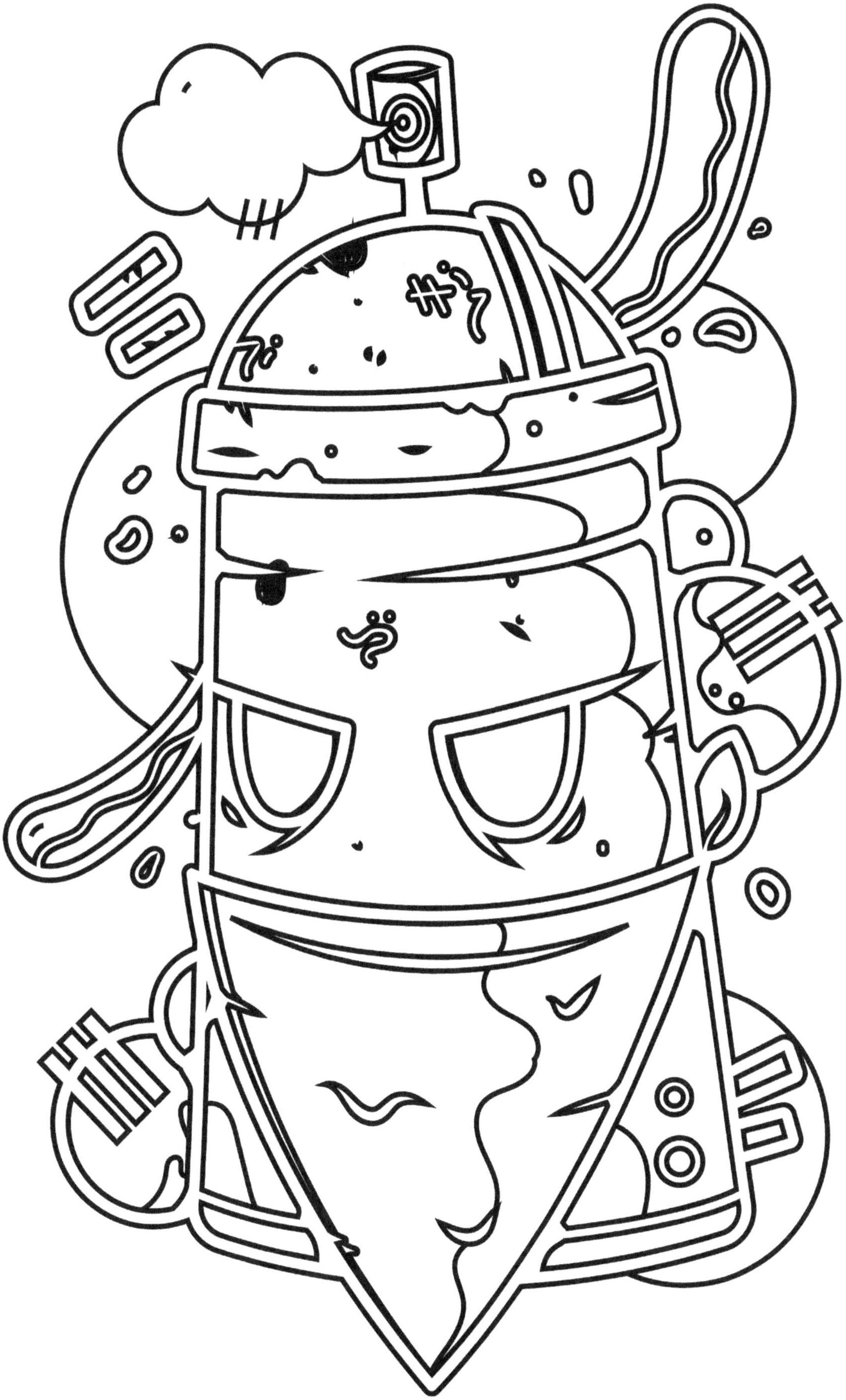

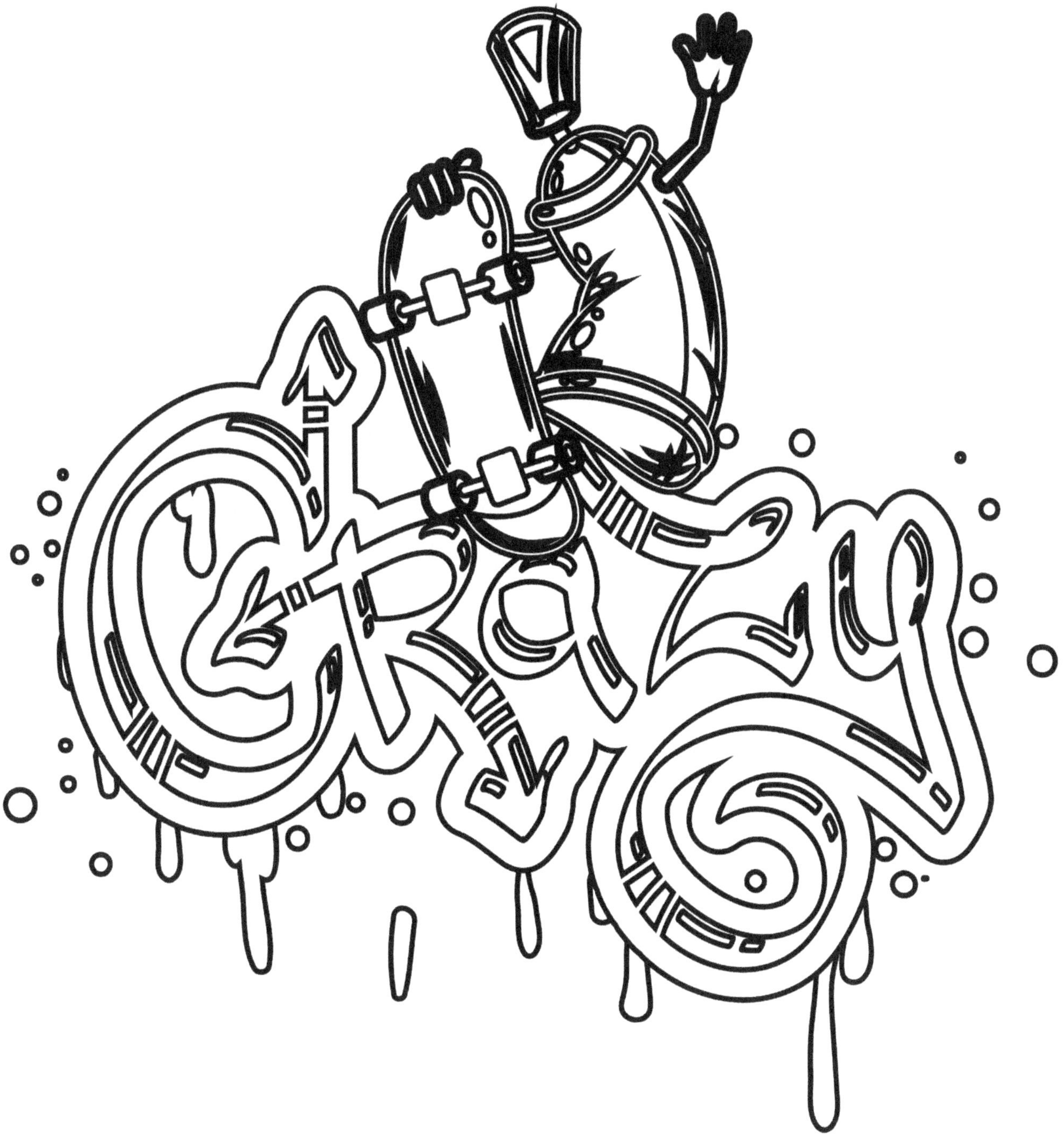
Crazy

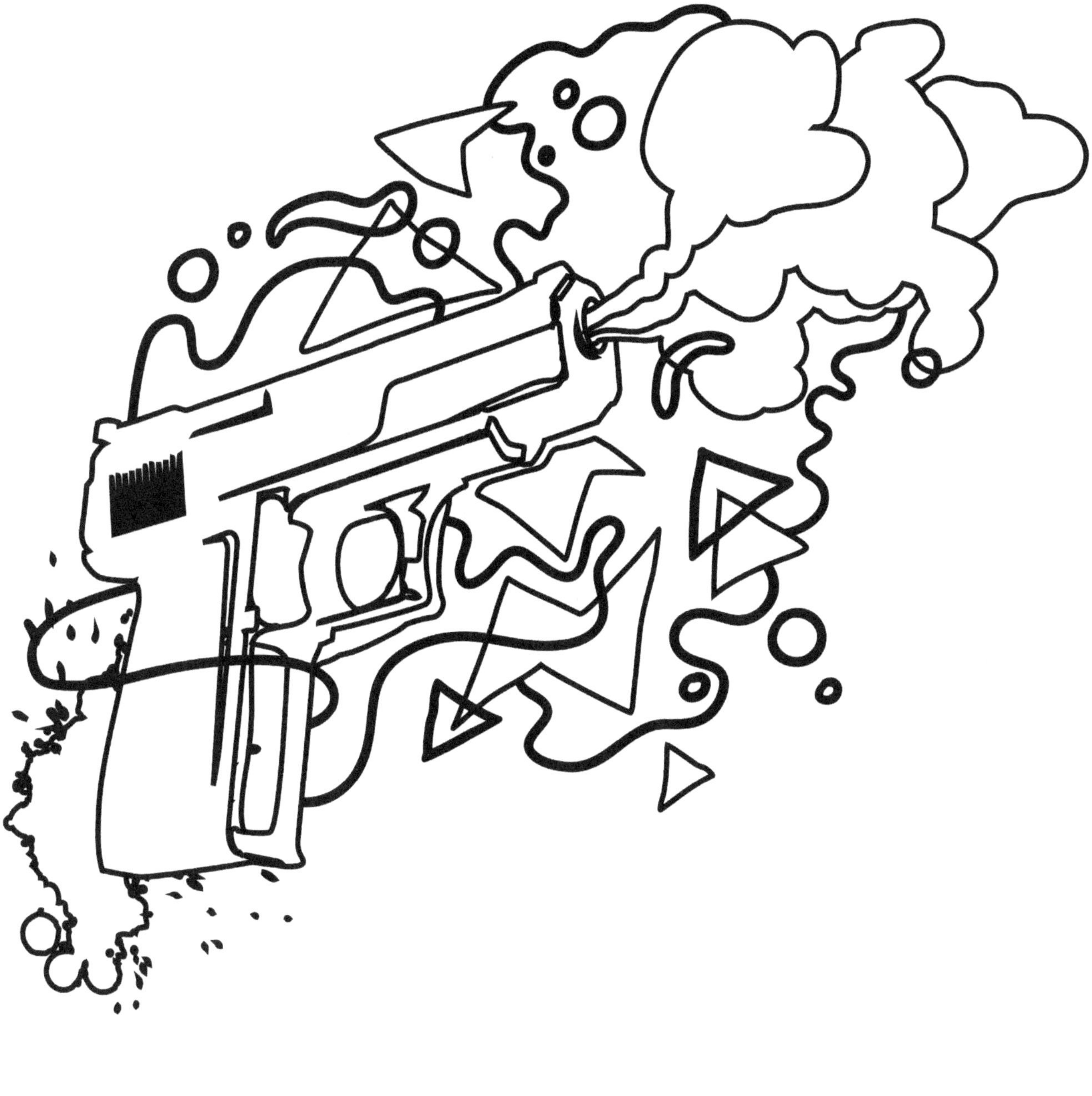

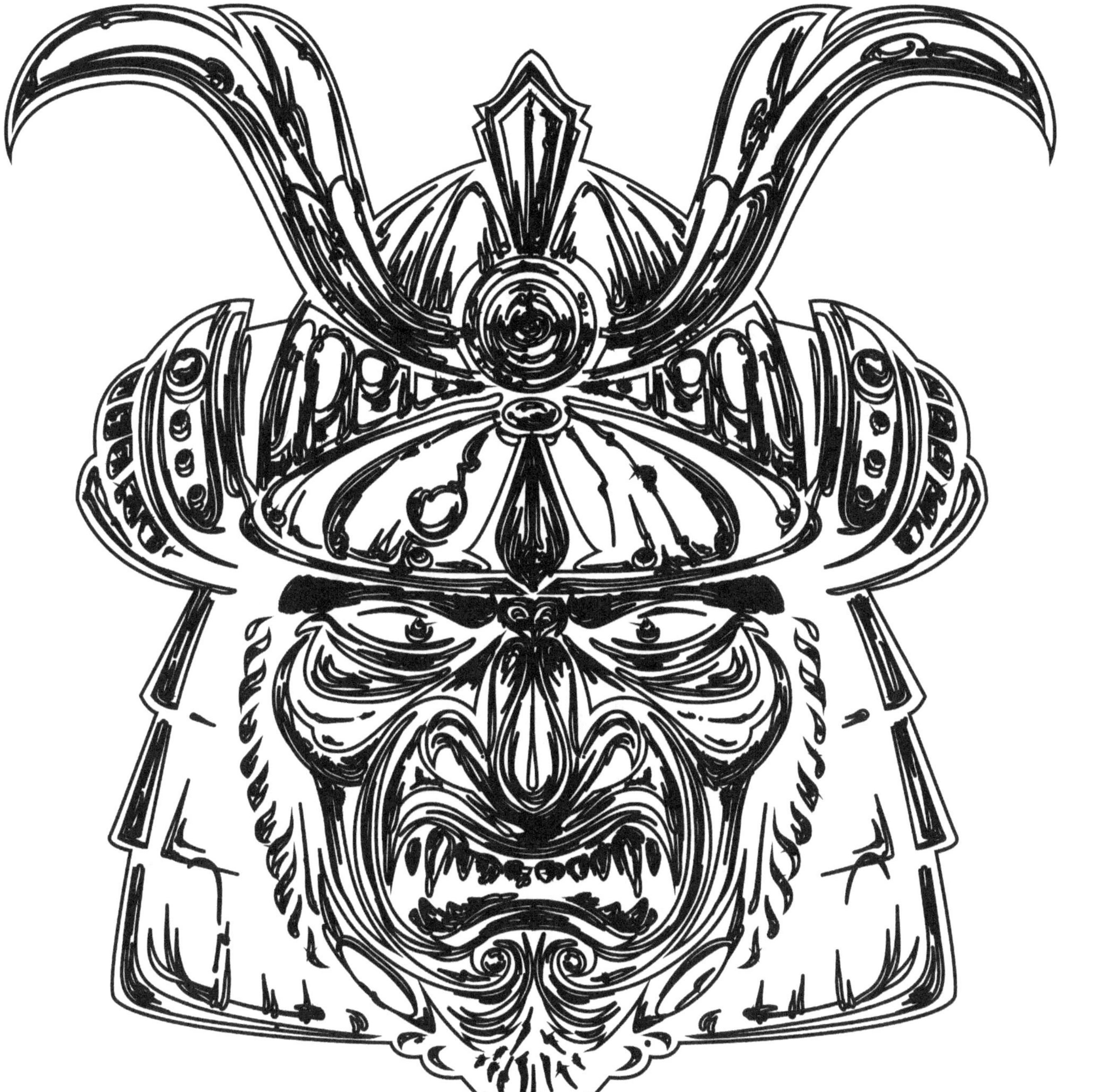

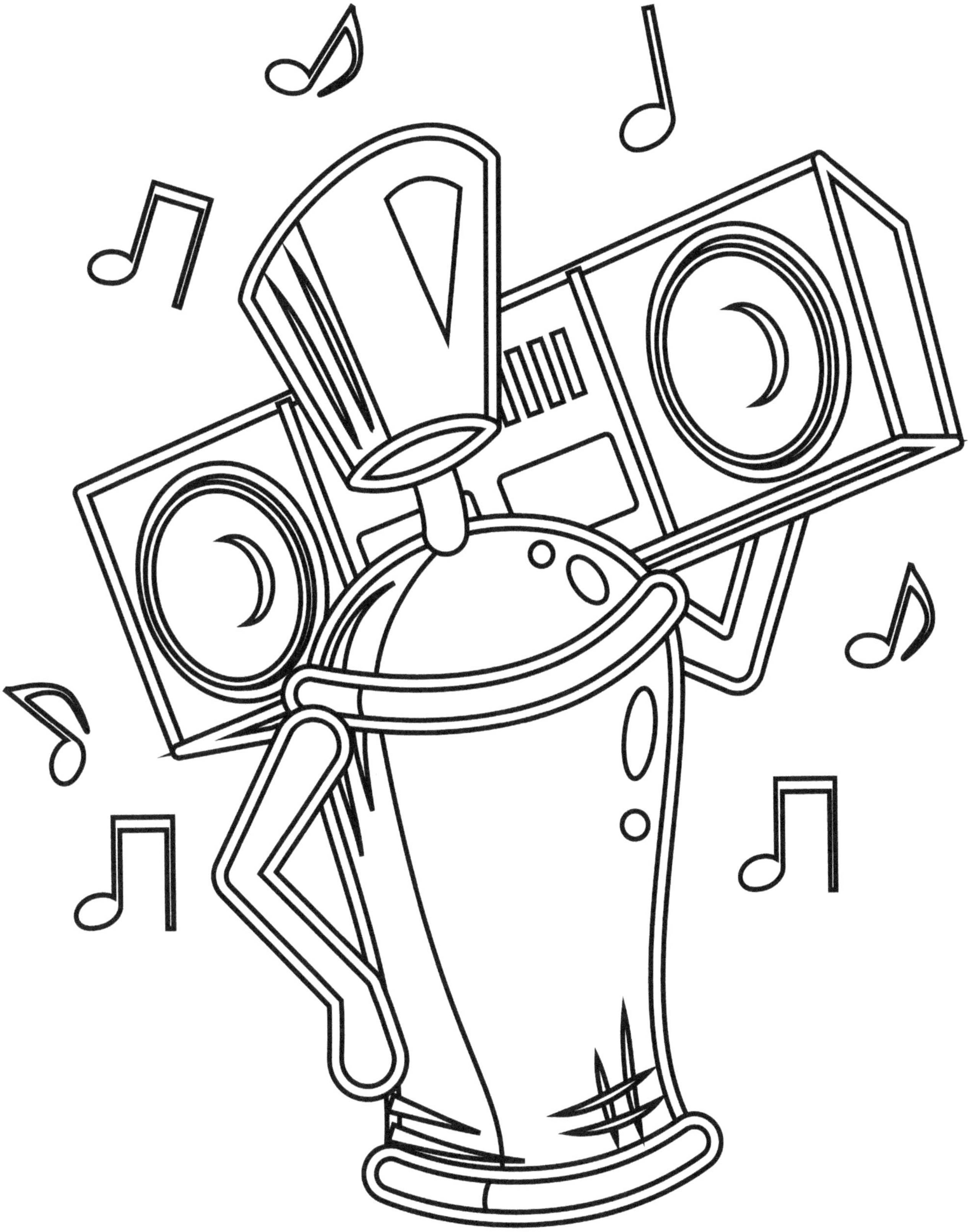

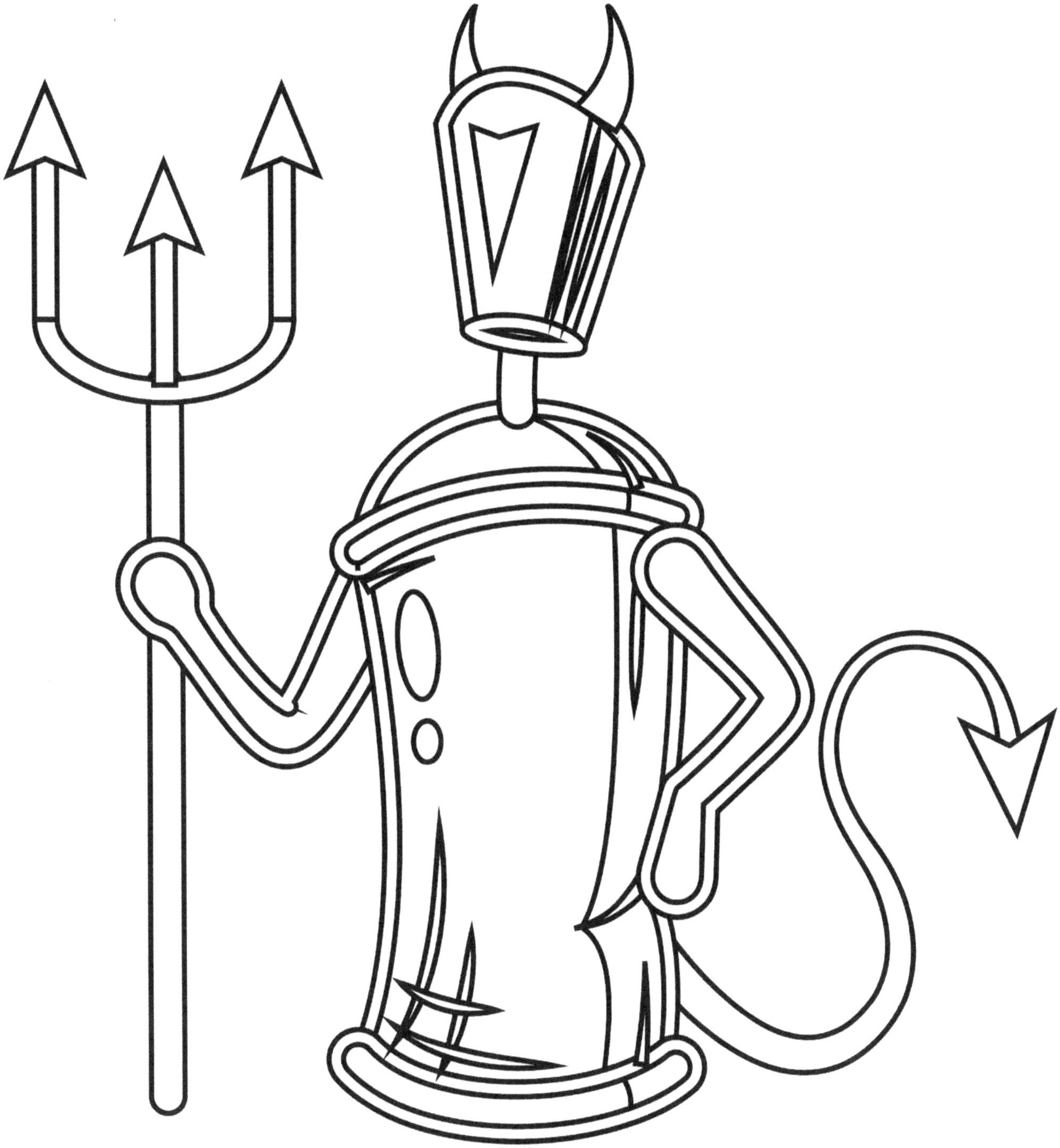

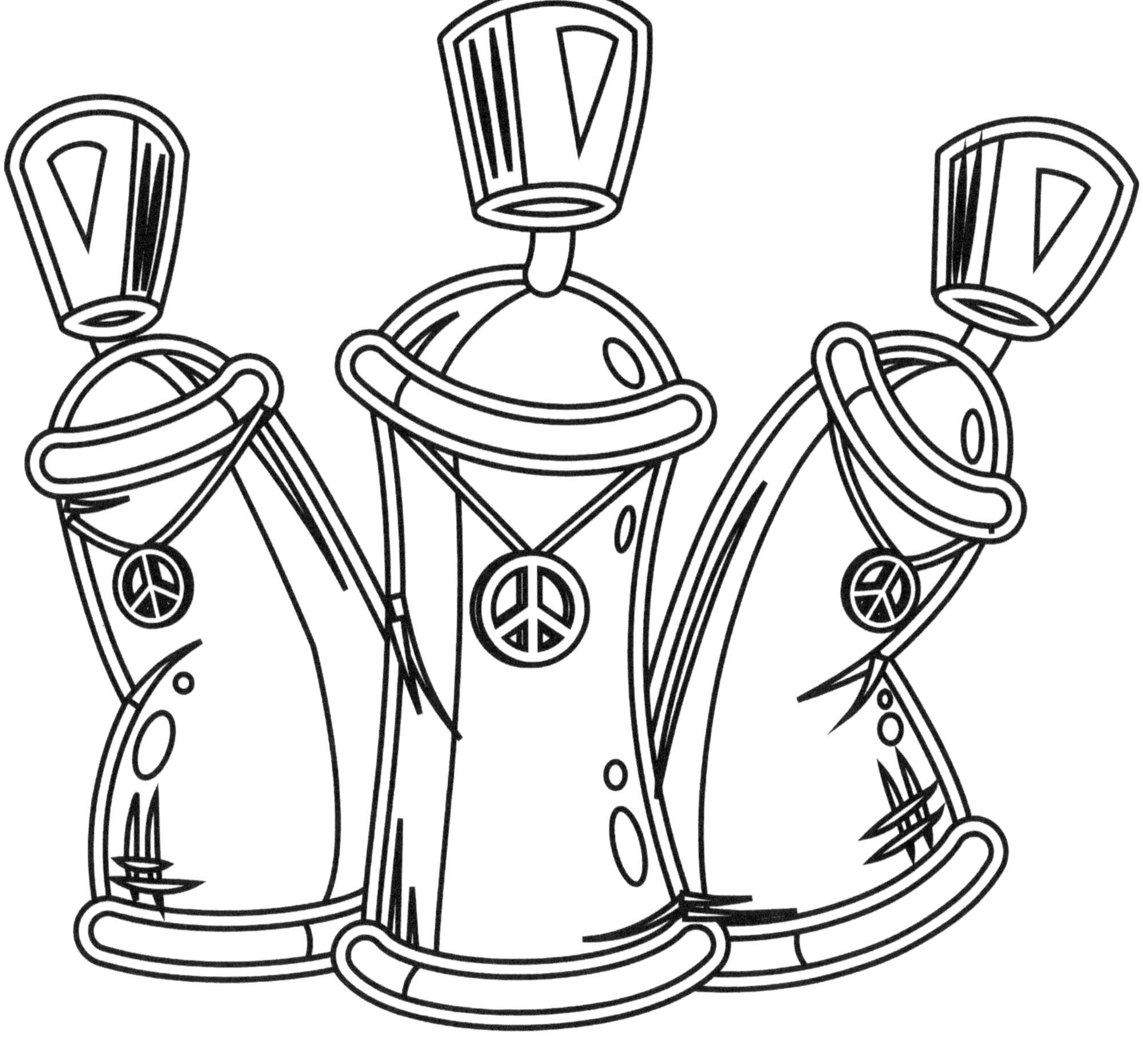

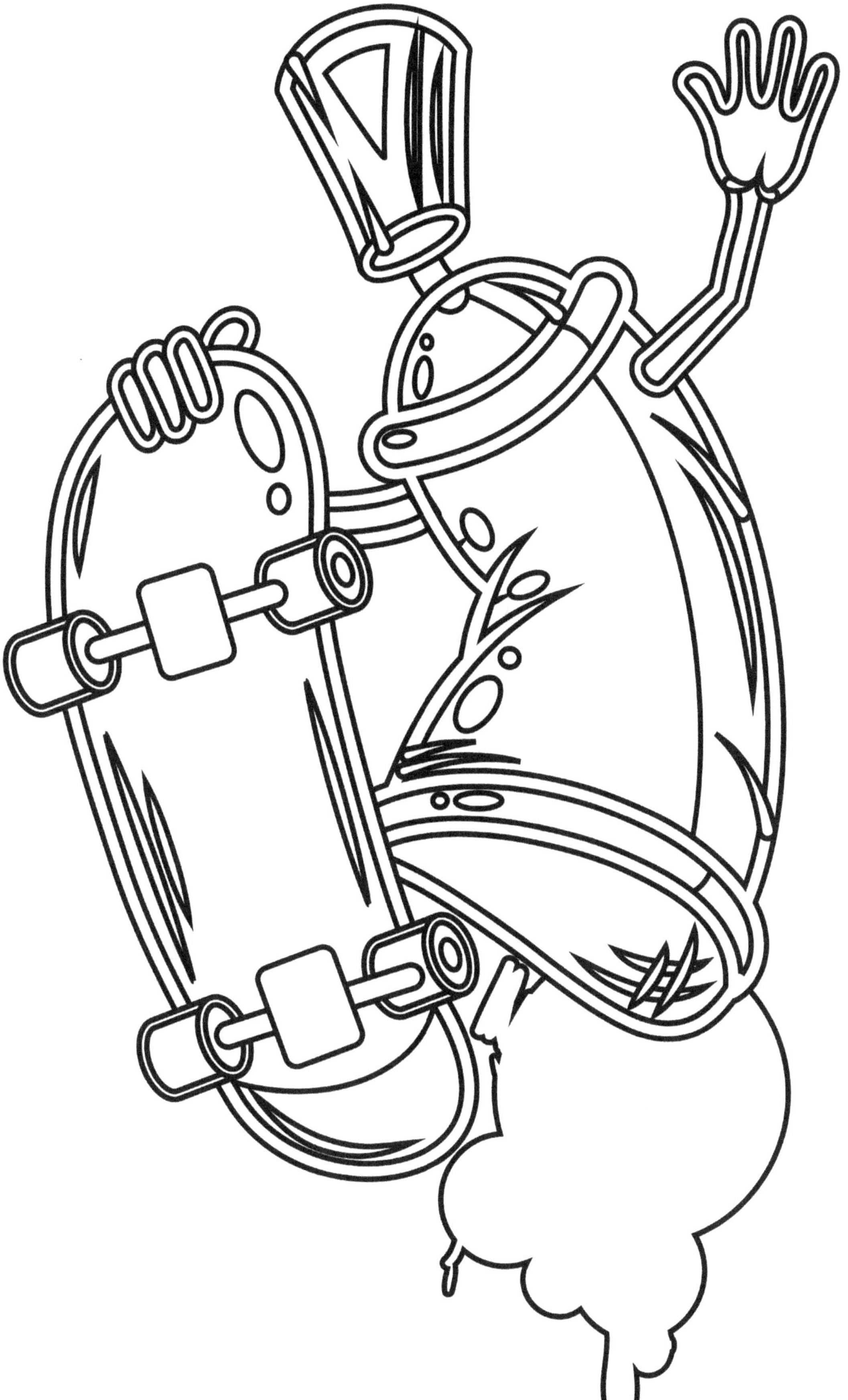

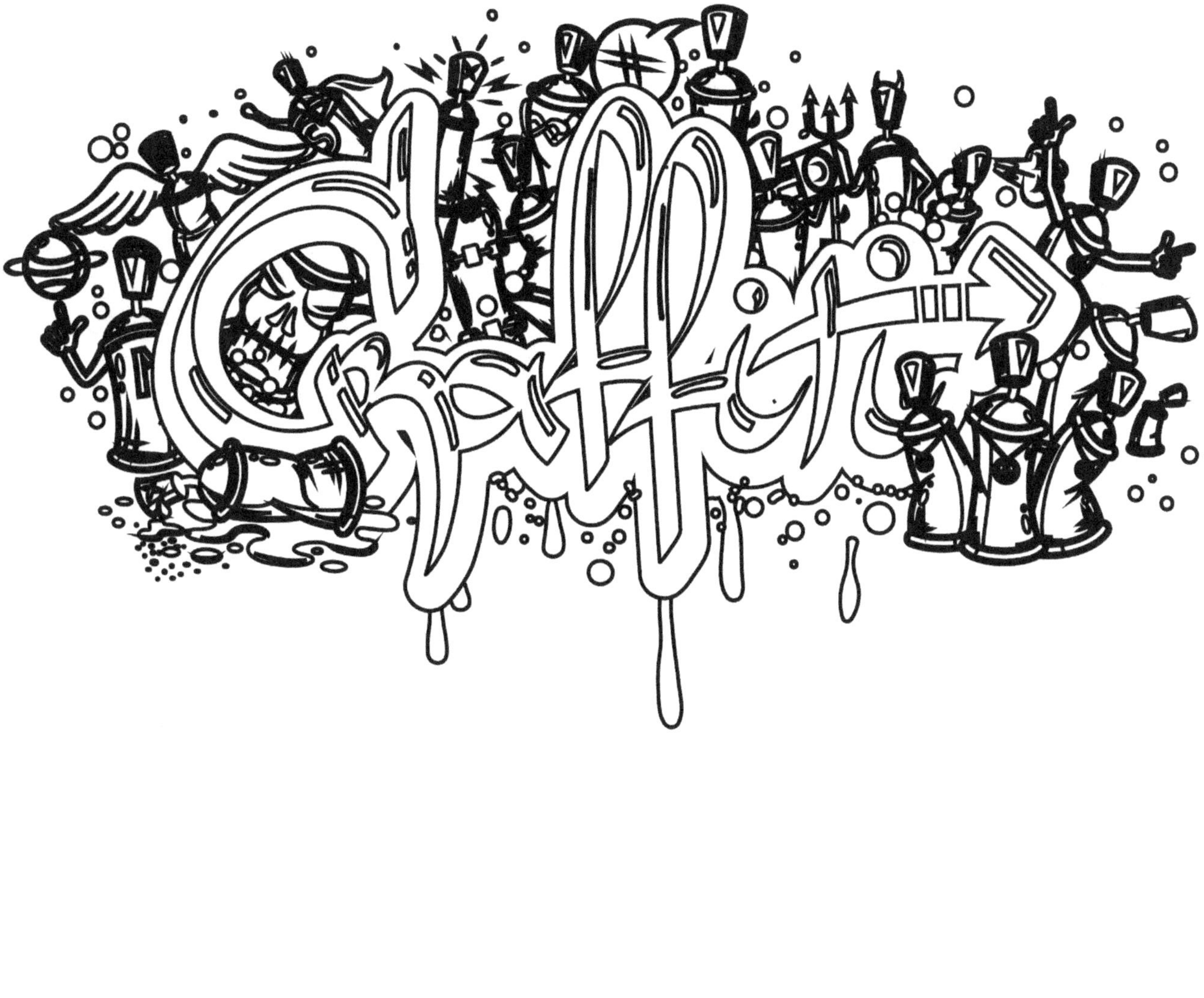

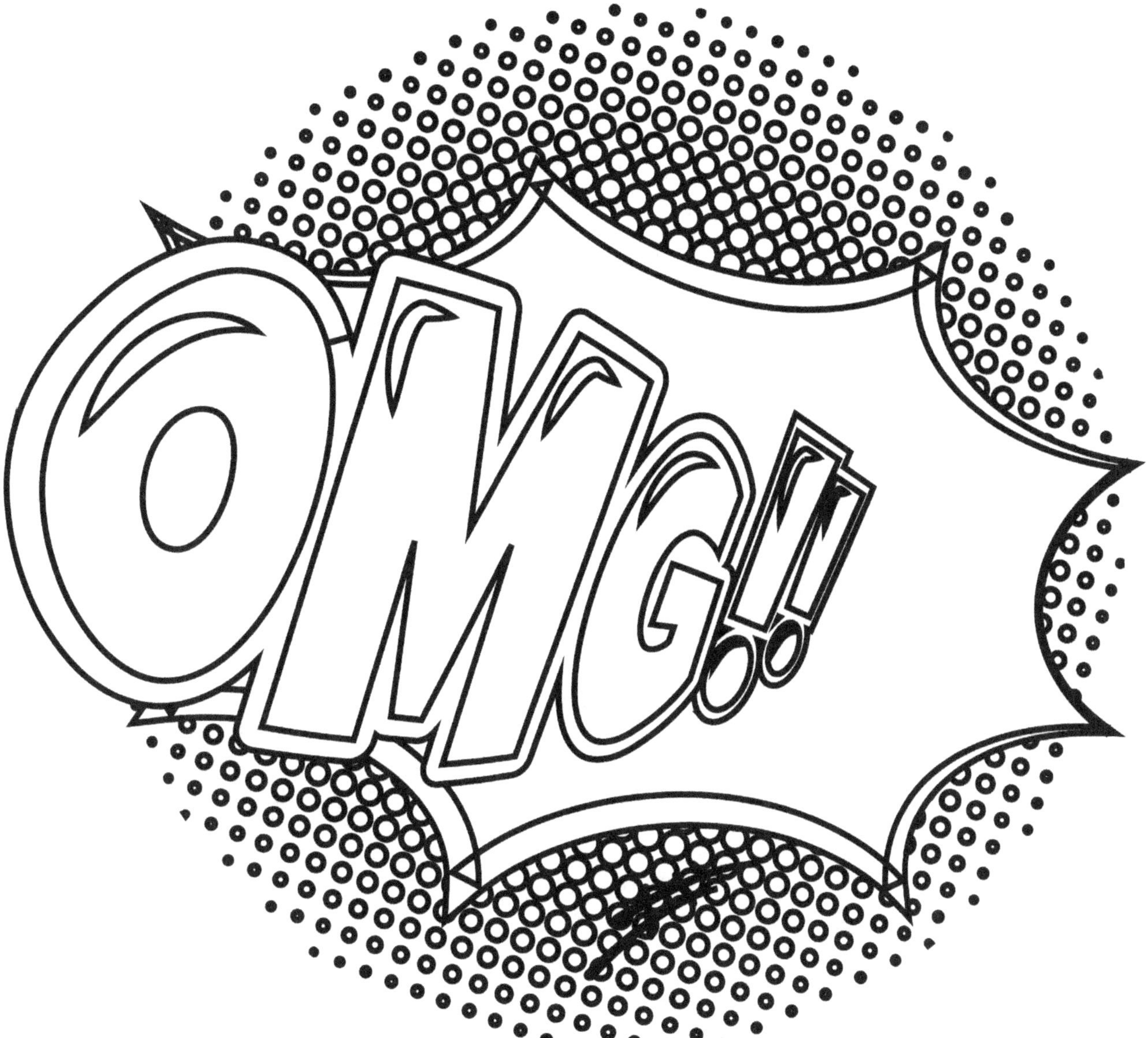
OMG!!

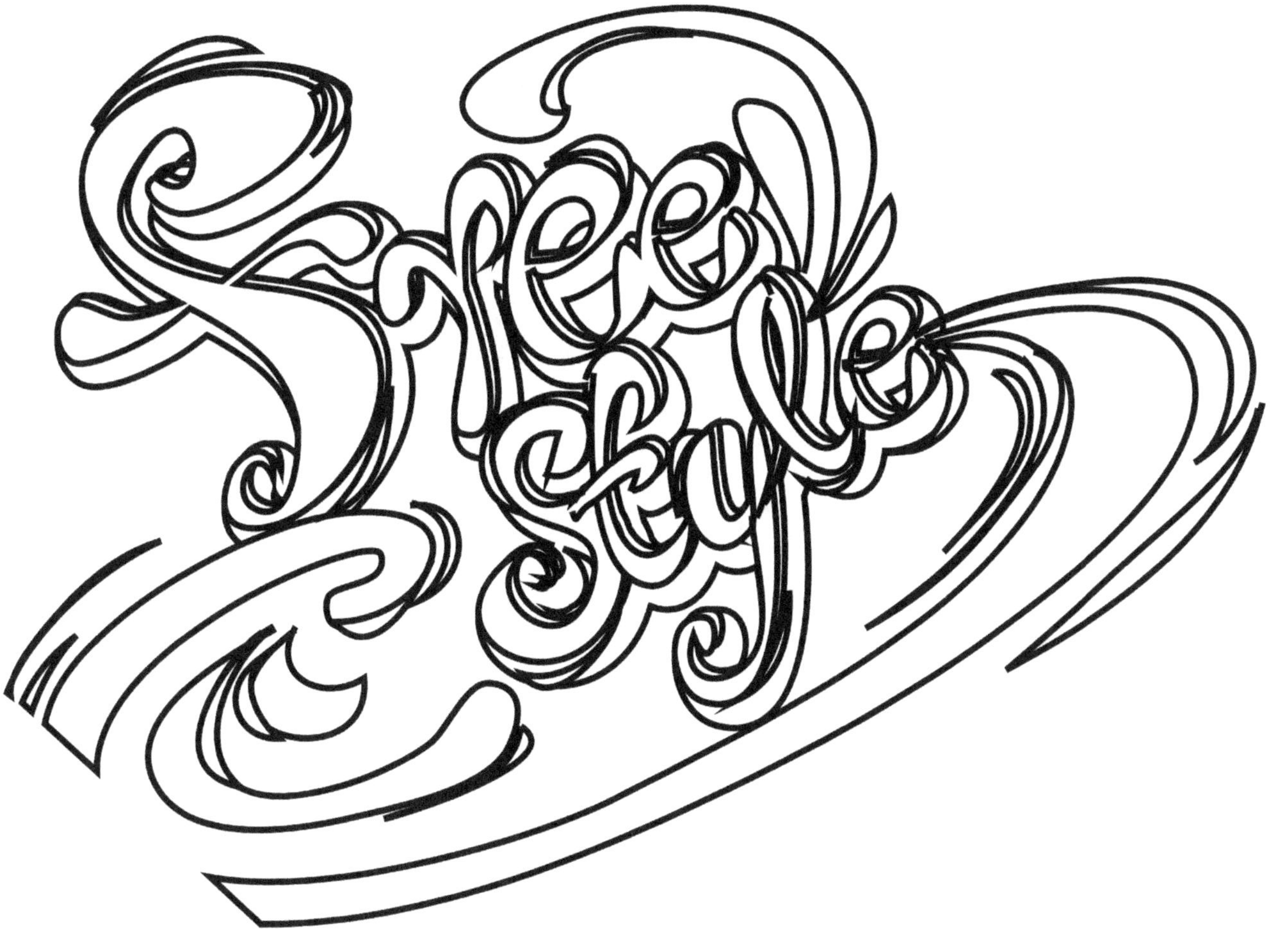
Free Style

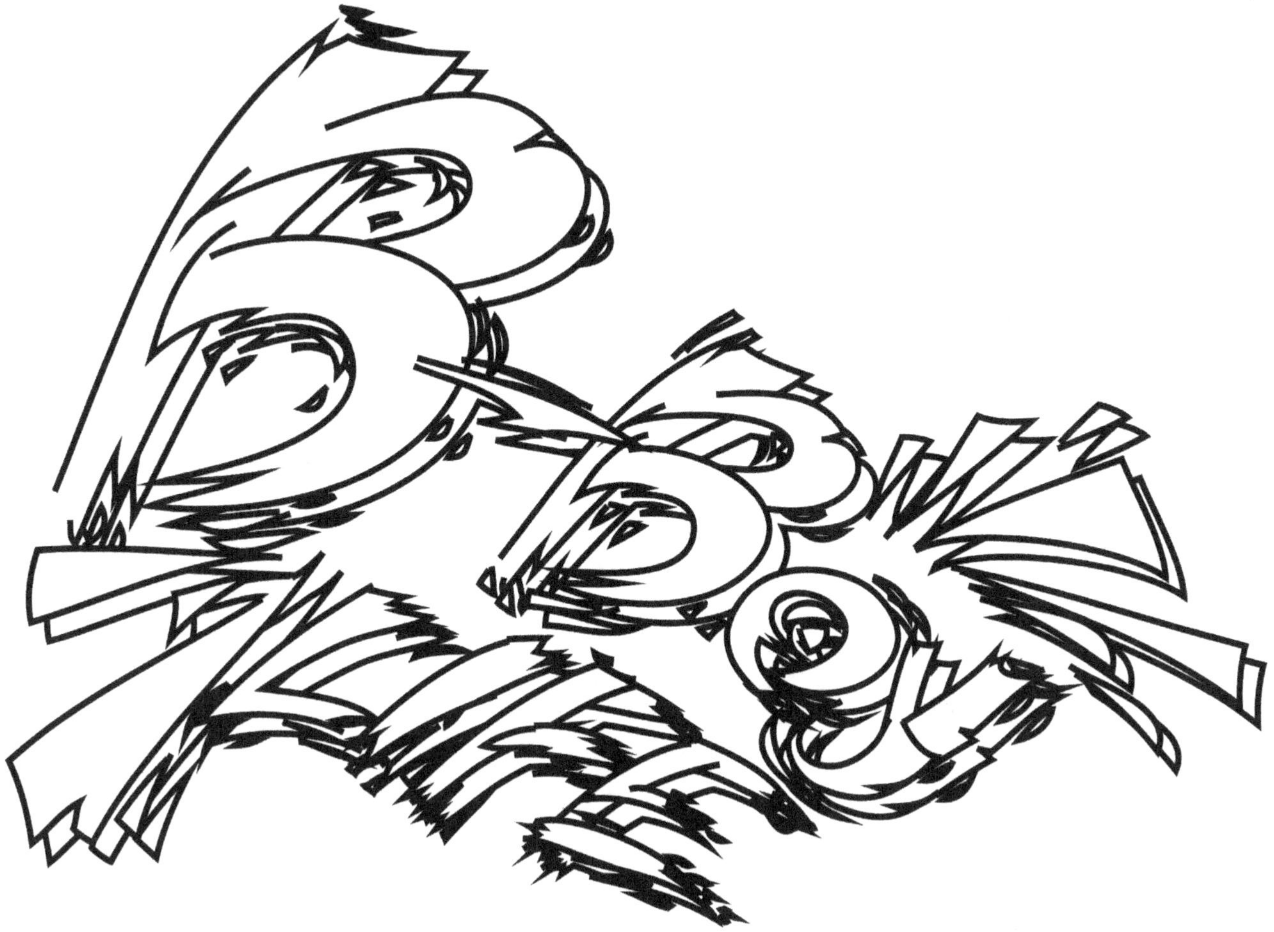

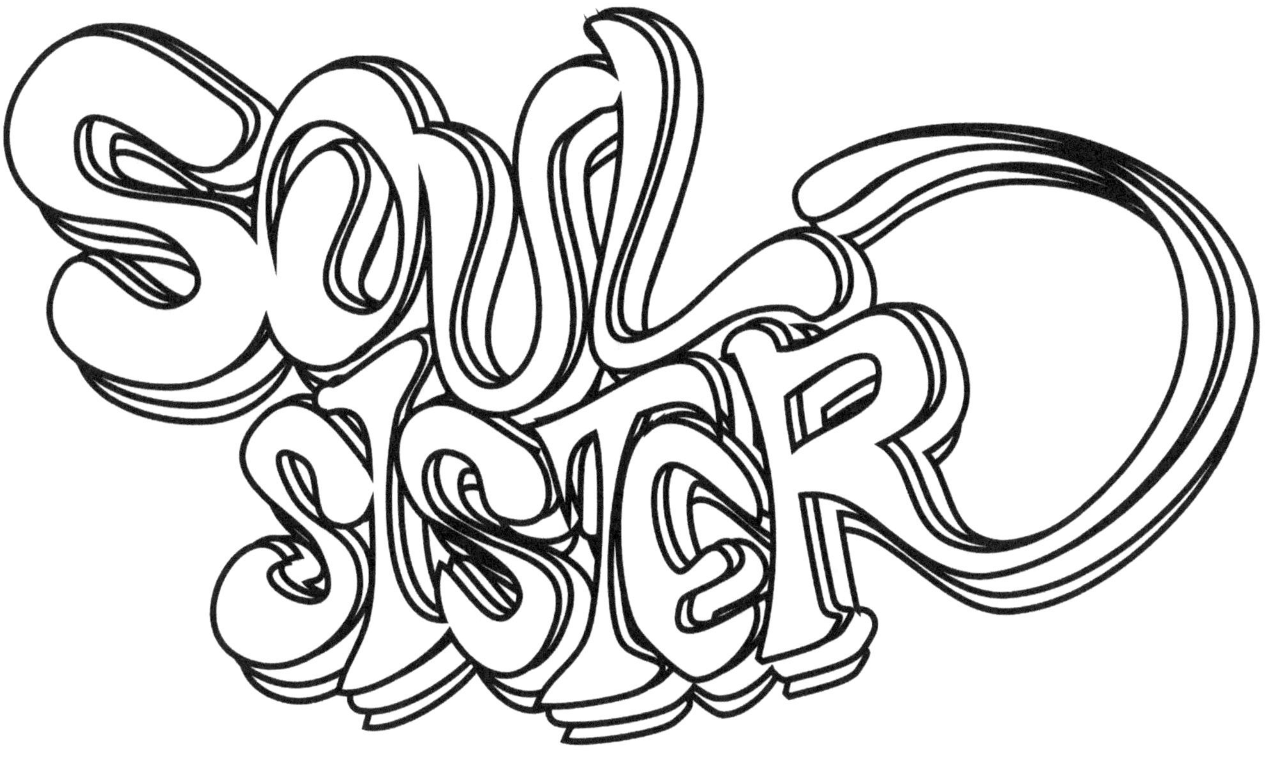
SOUL
SISTER

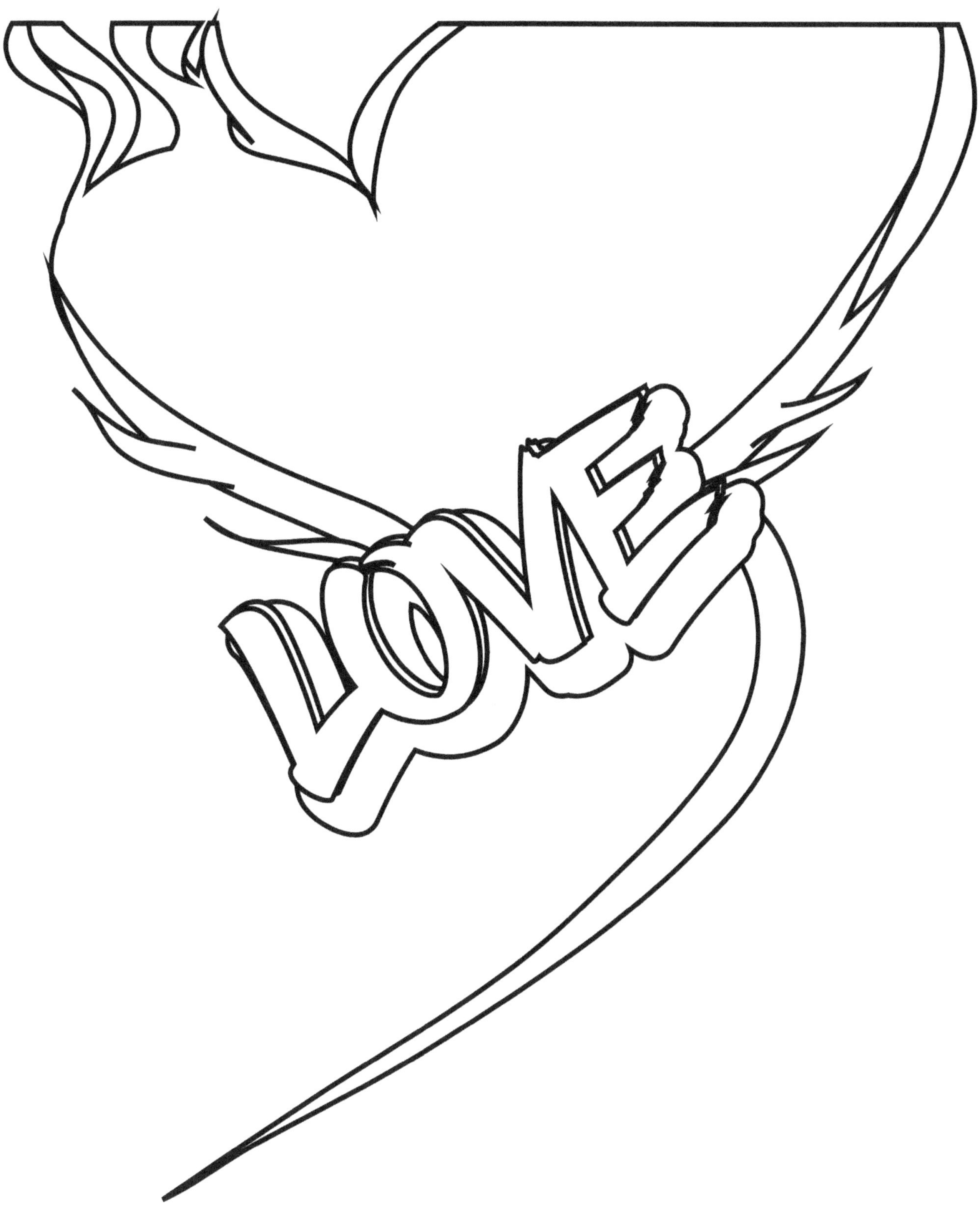
LOVE

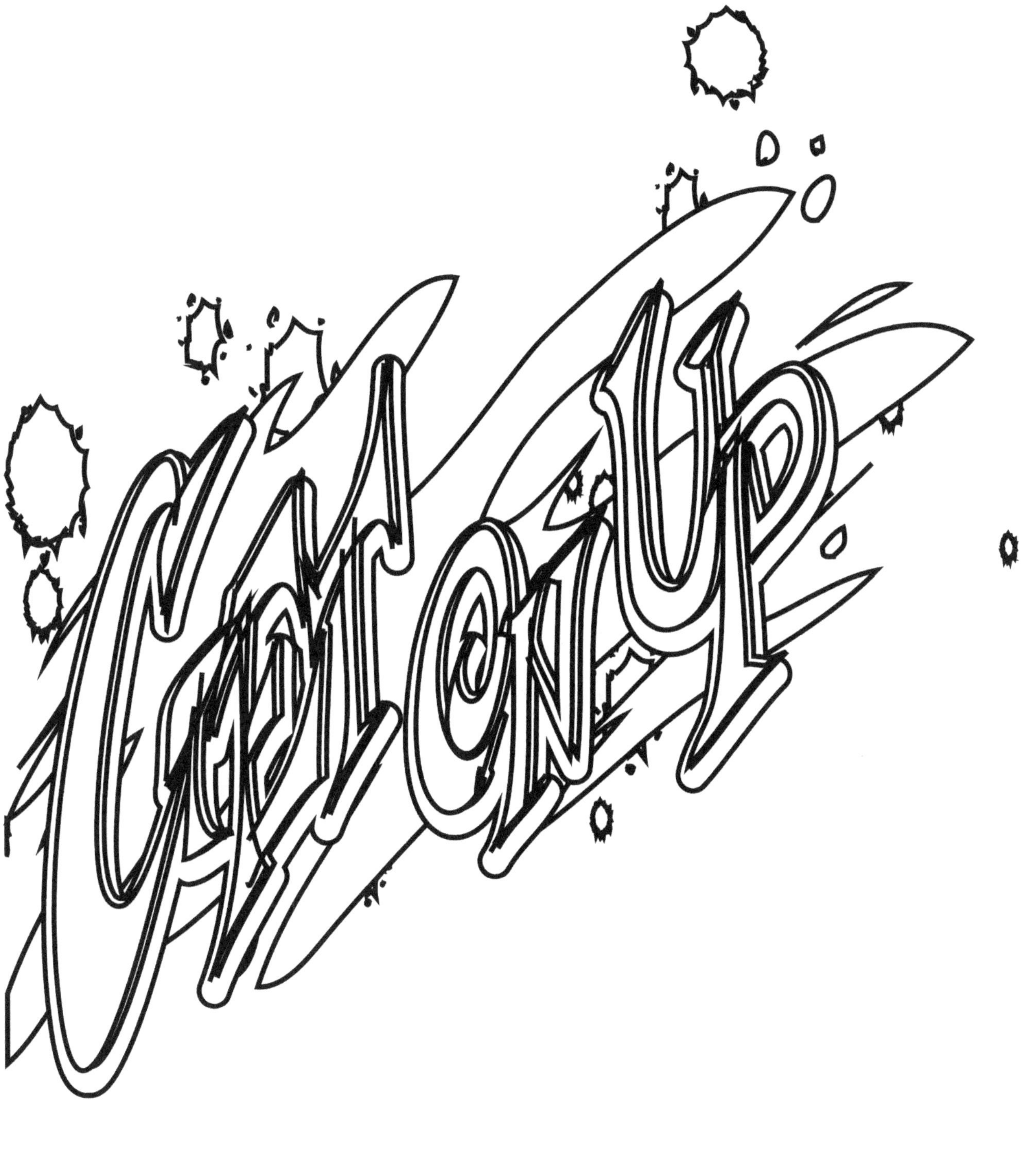

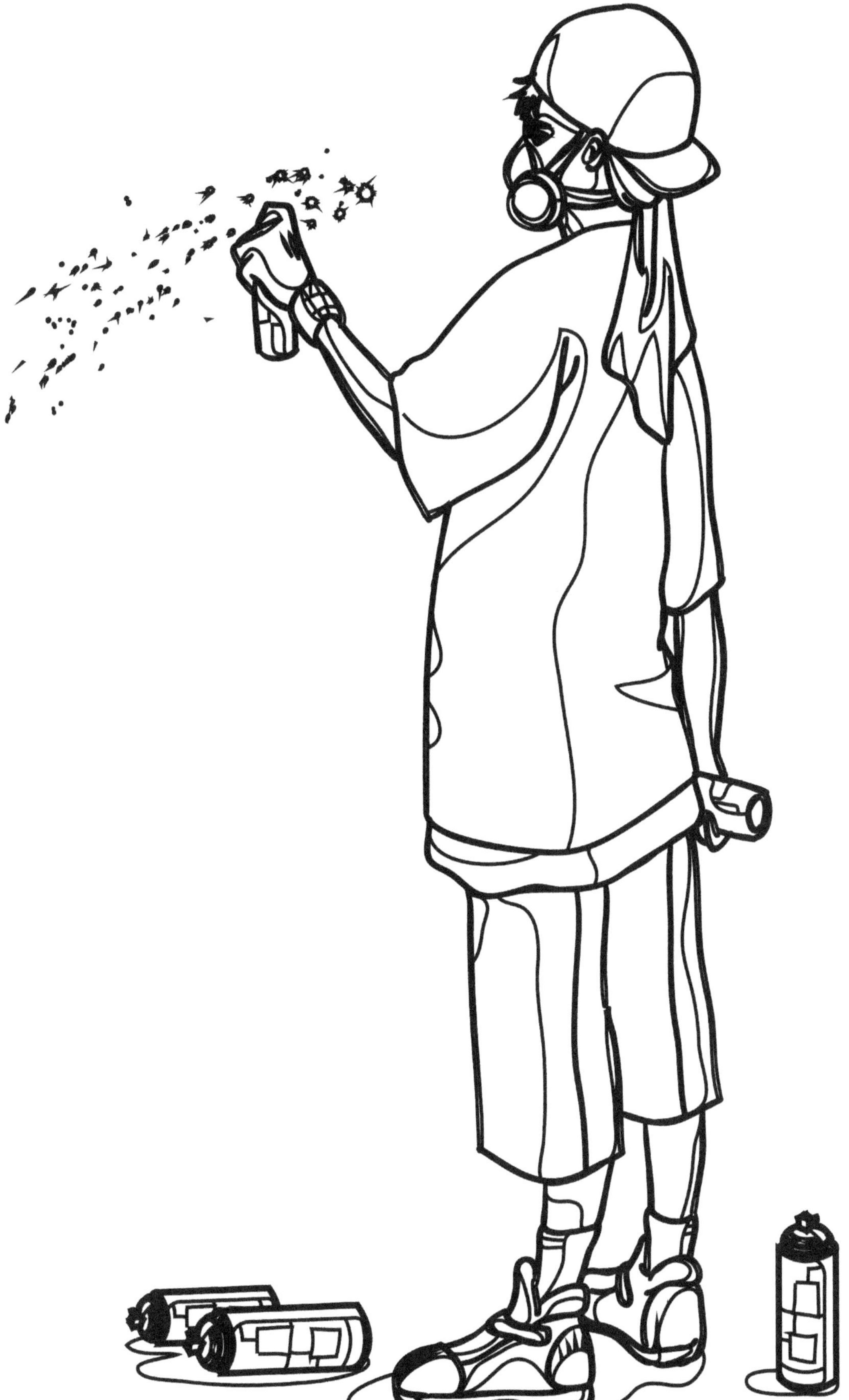

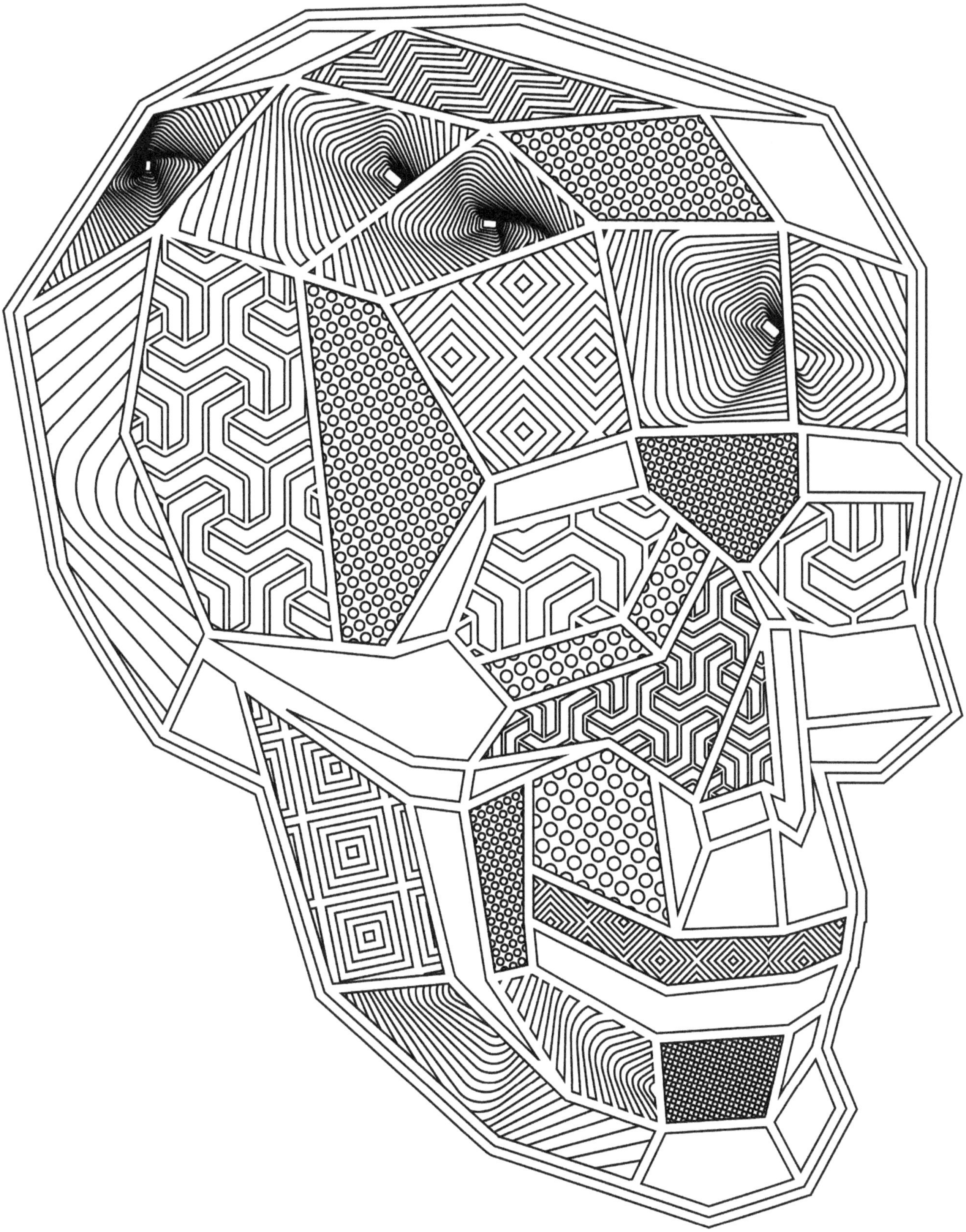

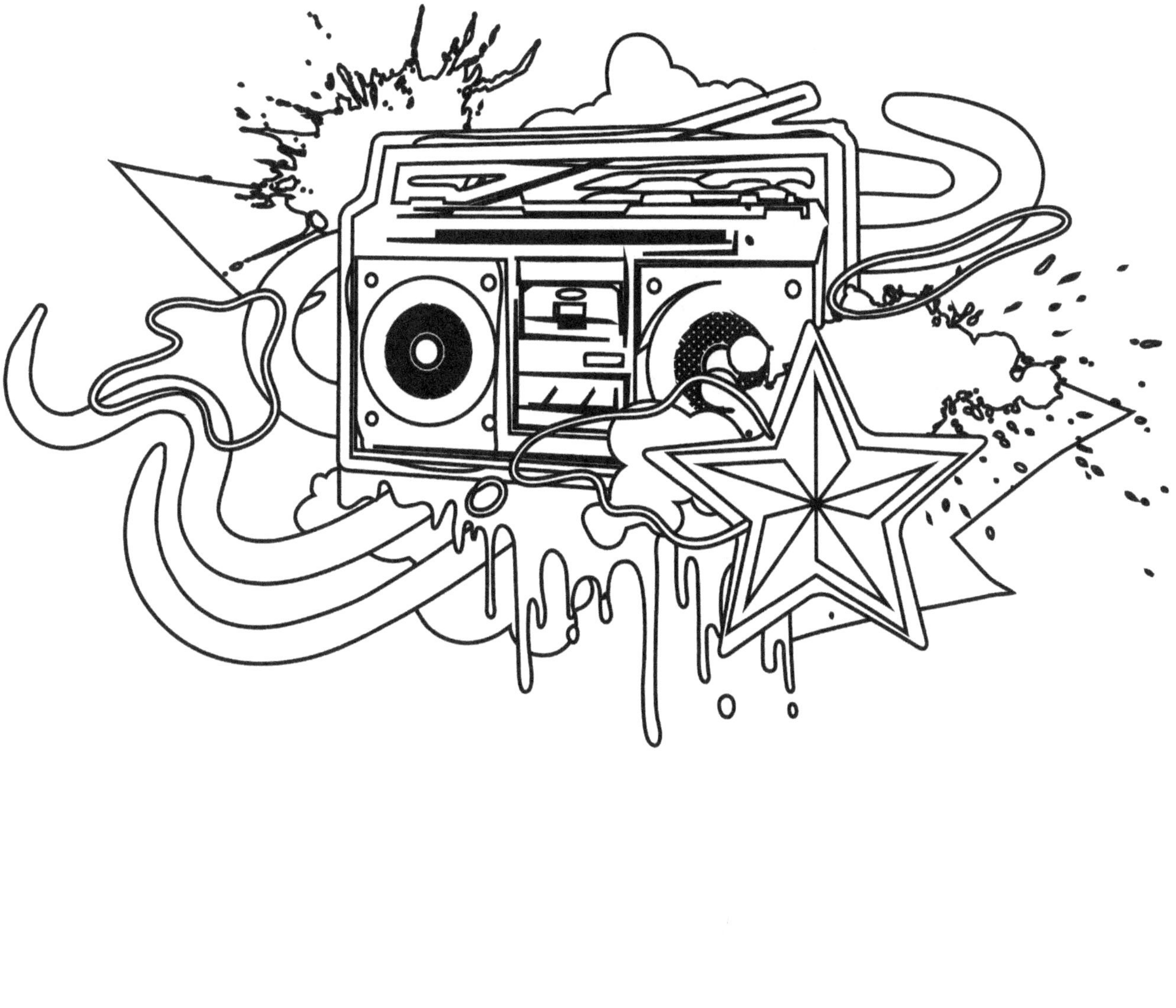

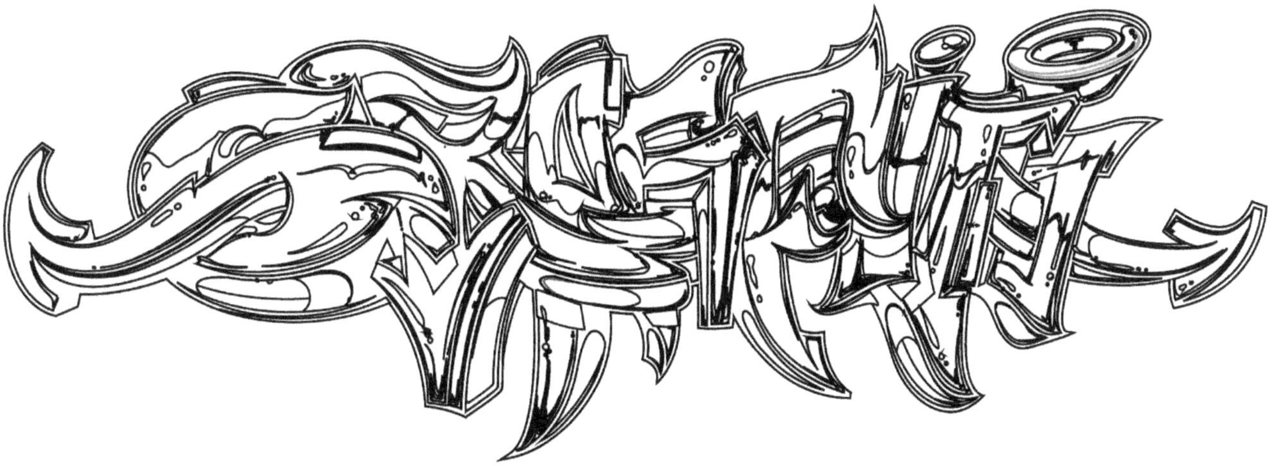

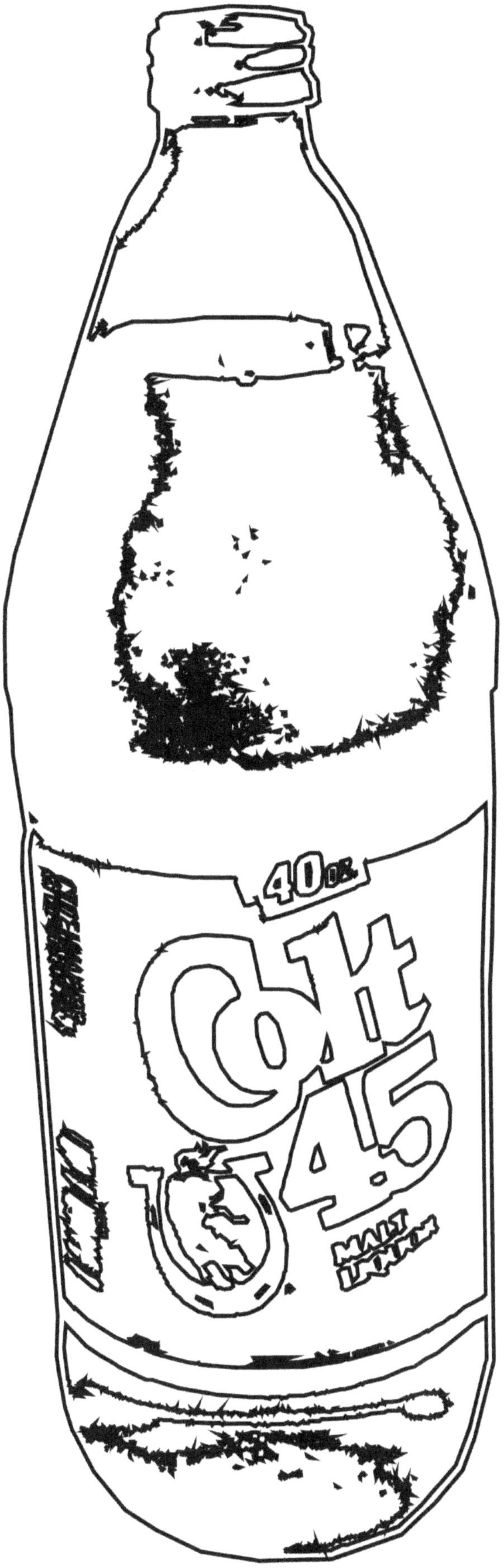
40
Colt
45
MALT

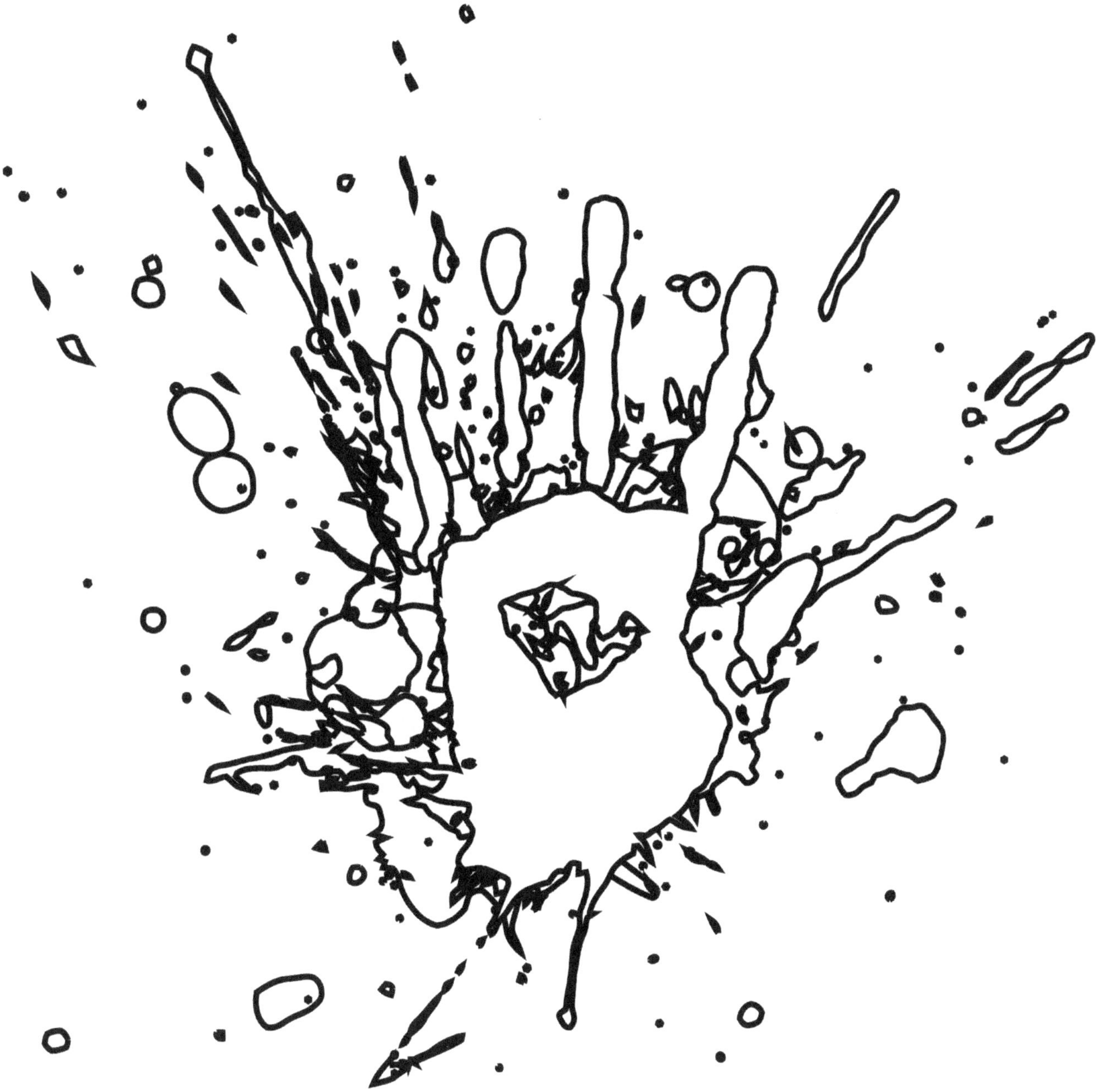

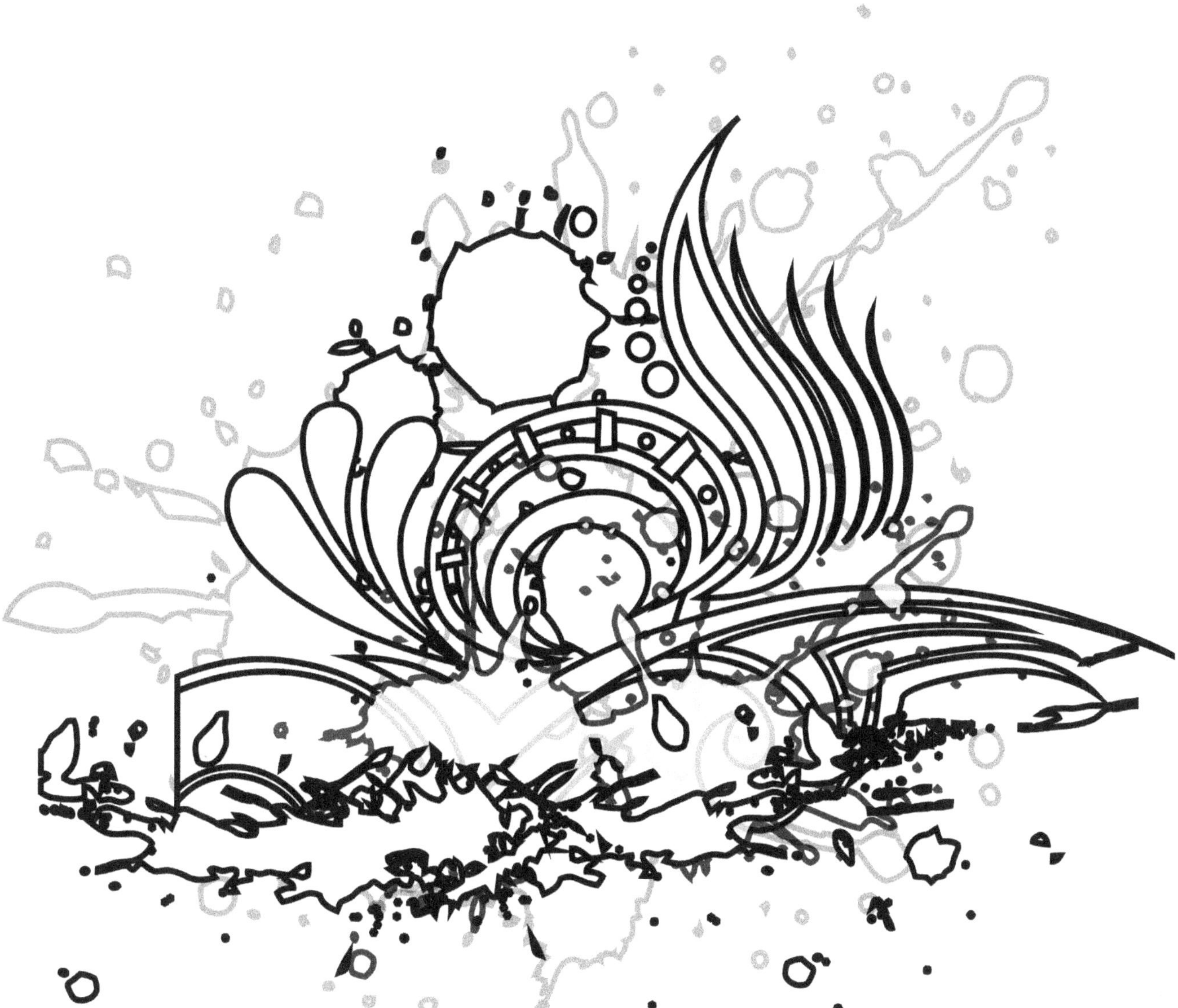

www.ingramcontent.com/pod-product-compliance
Lightning Source LLC
Chambersburg PA
CBHW081657220526
45466CB00009B/2795